Singin' for Kids

by Roger Emerson

PLAYBACK+

Speed • Pitch • Balance • Loop

To access audio and video, visit:
www.halleonard.com/mylibrary

Enter Code
8273-1606-2757-5241

ISBN 978-1-70514-482-4

HAL•LEONARD®

Copyright © 2023 by HAL LEONARD LLC
International Copyright Secured All Rights Reserved

Visit Hal Leonard Online at
www.halleonard.com

World headquarters, contact:
Hal Leonard
7777 West Bluemound Road
Milwaukee, WI 53213
Email: info@halleonard.com

In Europe, contact:
Hal Leonard Europe Limited
1 Red Place
London, W1K 6PL
Email: info@halleonardeurope.com

In Australia, contact:
Hal Leonard Australia Pty. Ltd.
4 Lentara Court
Cheltenham, Victoria, 3192 Australia
Email: info@halleonard.com.au

Introduction

SINGING IS FUN! The best part is that you can do it anywhere and your voice doesn't cost anything! It's a real instrument, you know, and this book will help you use it to the fullest! Like any activity or sport, the more you practice the better you become. EVERYONE can be a good singer and using this book will really help. When you feel confident, don't be afraid to sing for your family and friends or at school or church. I hope you have as much fun with this book as I did writing it!

READY, SET, SING!

Roger Emerson

How to Use this Book

Print and Interactive Content

- 12 songs that are perfect for young singers are included

- Each song will contain a short lesson on singing or music fundamentals

- Since singing is often a "by ear" activity, we are including both lyric sheets and notation lead sheets for each song

- The price of this book includes access to video and audio tracks online, for download or streaming, using the unique code found on page 1

- Entering that code will take you to "My Library," where you will find both lyrics highlighted and synced with audio as well as music and lyrics synced with demonstration audio

- Audio tracks of accompaniment are included for performance

- We have included a section of the basics of reading music and vocal production as well. Pages 3-9 are adapted from *Sight-Reading for Young Singers* by Emily Crocker (HL00388201).

SECTION 1: Reading Music

GIVE ME THE BEAT!

Beat is a steady recurring pulse, like a heartbeat. Tap or clap with a metronome. You can access demonstration metronome beats on the MyLibrary page, using the code found on page 1.

TEMPO

The speed of the beat, faster or slower, is called *tempo*.

Try clapping along with the metronome again. When you change the metronome setting, you change the tempo.

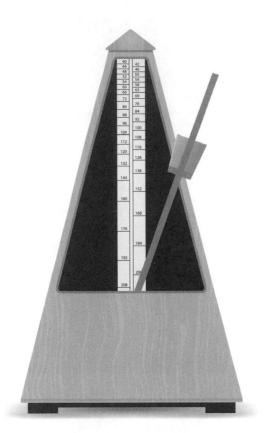

The number stands for "beats per minute" or "bpm."
Try a different tempo and see if you can clap it accurately.

100 bpm	92 bpm
120 bpm	88 bpm
132 bpm	72 bpm
144 bpm	60 bpm

Choose your own tempo!

MEET THE NOTES

A *note* represents musical sound. The length (duration) of the sound is represented by different note values. Here are three note values:

quarter
note

half
note

whole
note

The following chart represents four beats of sound, with **four quarter notes** having the same duration as **two half notes** or **one whole note**.

The combination of different note values is called *rhythm*.

Read Quarter Notes

The **quarter note** is commonly assigned the beat. Practice reading **quarter notes** by chanting the syllable "da" while tapping the beat.

da da da da da da da da da da da da da da da da

Read Half Notes

A *half note* is two beats of sound. Practice reading *half notes* by chanting the syllables "da-a" while tapping the beat.

da - a   da - a   da - a   da - a   da - a   da - a   da - a   da - a

Read Whole Notes

A *whole note* receives four beats of sound. Practice reading *whole notes* by chanting the syllables "da-a-a-a" while tapping the beat.

da - a - a - a   da - a - a - a   da - a - a - a   da - a - a - a

MEASURE, METER, AND BARLINE

Rhythm can be organized with *barlines* and *measures*. A *barline* is a vertical line that separates rhythm into smaller sections called *measures*.

A *double barline* is placed at the end of a section or piece of music.

Measures and barlines are organized by *meter*. The numbers that identify the meter are called the *time signature* and are placed at the beginning of a song or section of a song.

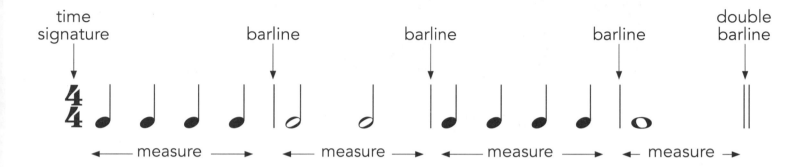

TIME SIGNATURES

Here are three common time signatures:

4 = four beats per measure
4 = quarter note receives the beat

3 = three beats per measure
4 = quarter note receives the beat

2 = two beats per measure
4 = quarter note receives the beat

LET'S MAKE MELODY!

Pitch refers to the highness or lowness of musical sound. Music notes are another name for pitch. Music notes are identified by the first seven letters of the alphabet, from A to G.

The piano keyboard is organized by groups of two and three black keys. The white key to the left of a group of two black keys is always C. The C nearest the middle of the keyboard is called *Middle C*.

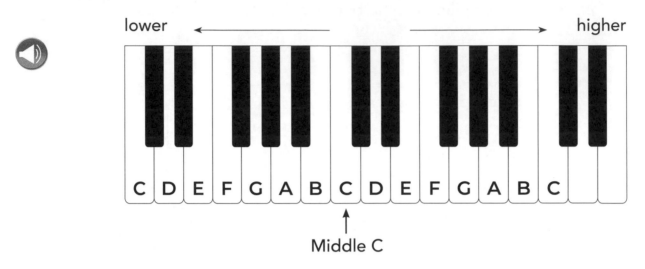

Music is written on a staff of five lines and four spaces.

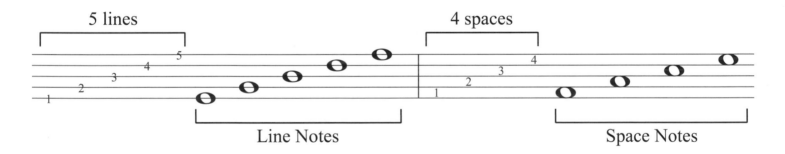

Some notes are written on a line.

line note

Some notes are written on a space.

space note

NOTES ON THE STAFF

The symbol at the beginning of the left side of the staff is called a **treble clef**. Middle C has its own little line below the treble staff called a **ledger** line. Ledger lines can be used below or above a staff.

Treble clef

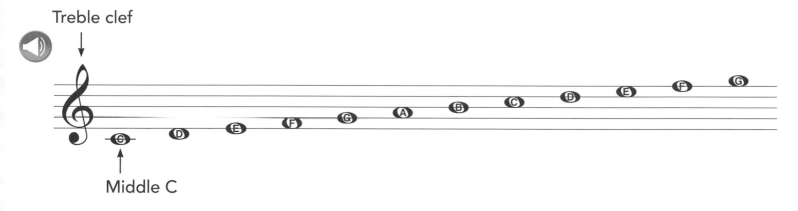

Middle C

A **scale** is a group of pitches lower and higher. Play a scale on a keyboard starting on C and ending on C, using only the white keys and without skipping any keys. This forms a pattern of pitches called a **major scale**.

C Major Scale

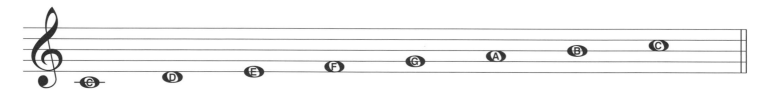

Another way to name pitches is by using **solfège**, a method for singing melodies using Latin note names.

C Major Scale with Solfege

do   re   mi   fa   sol   la   ti   do

SECTION 2: The Voice

Your voice is a real instrument. It has three basic parts.

1. The lungs

2. The vocal folds

3. The mouth and face

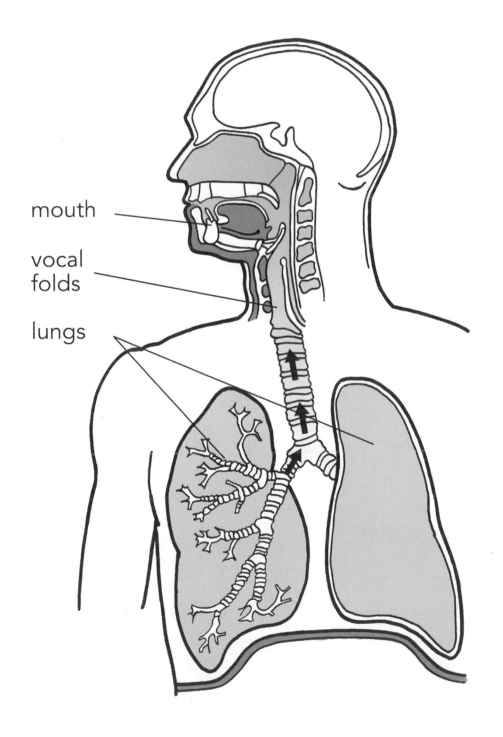

mouth

vocal folds

lungs

Posture
(Holding Your Singing Instrument)

- Stand tall.

- Feet are slightly apart with your strong foot slightly forward.

- Arms are at your sides, unless you are holding a microphone or gesturing during a song.

Breath
(Using Your Air for Singing)

- Put your hands on your hips like a superhero.

- Take a deep breath and feel your waist expand.

- Hiss all your air out like a snake! (Hsssssssss)

- Take another full breath and blow it out as if you are whistling but don't make a sound. This is the feeling you need whenever you sing a line of music. We call it "breath control."

Making a Sound
(We call it "Phonation")

With posture in place…

- Take a deep breath.

- Yawn and sigh from high to low. Do this several times.

- Make a sound like a siren from a firetruck.

- Buzz your lips like a motorboat. (I'll bet you've done this in a pool or bathtub!)

- Buzz low to high, then high to low.

More sounds
(We call them "vocal warmups")

- Hee-haw like a donkey.

- Sigh from high to low again, but this time end with the word "yum" and hold it for as long as you can. Don't forget to take a big breath!

- Let's hum a downward scale (a ladder of notes)

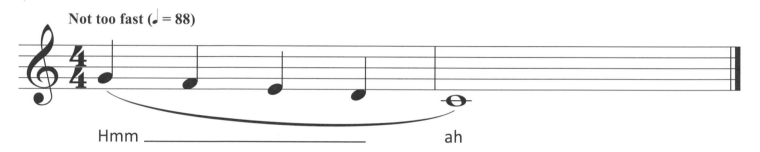

- Let's do it again, ending with an "ah" sound

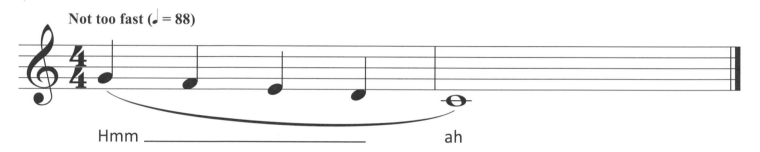

Hint: The curved line is called a **slur** which means the notes should be smooth and connected and sung on one breath.

More sounds (continued)

- Let's sing it higher! Up by a half step

Hint: The comma is a breath mark.
Take a breath!

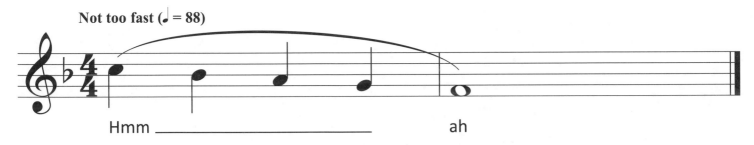

Sing it again a half step higher and repeat five times, moving up each time.

Here is where you will end! See how the notes are now higher in the staff?

- Bonus: go higher if you can!

More Warmups
Building Your Voice

- Exercise 5: moving from lower voice to upper voice smoothly

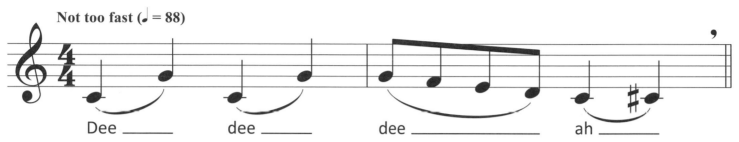

Dee _____ dee _____ dee _____ ah _____

Sing it again a half step higher and repeat five times, moving up each time.

- Exercise 6: expanding your range

Hah hah hah hah hah hah hah hah hah hah hah hah hah _____

Sing it again a half step higher and repeat five times, moving up each time.

- Exercise 7: shaping tall vowels for beautiful singing

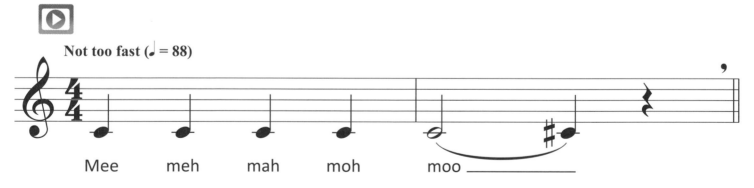

Mee meh mah moh moo _____

Sing it again a half step higher and repeat five times, moving up each time.

- Exercise 8: Flexing Your Articulators

Say: "Sit on a potato pan Otis." Do it four times quickly. Can you say it backwards? It's a palindrome, which is the same backwards and forward!

SECTION 3: Songs

Let's Sing!
Using all we have learned from the videos:

- Posture—stand straight and tall

- Breath—breathe deeply before each line of music

- Phonation—make beautiful sounds with your voice

- Reading words and music—follow the lyrics and the notes

Let's move ahead on our own with real songs! Our first new concept is *expression*.

Happy

DESCRIPTION & INSTRUCTION

Expression: using your face and eyes to tell the story of the song.

- Fun fact: the artist and composer Pharrell Williams is also a fashion designer and has a son named Rocket!

- Look at the words of this song. Are they happy? Sad? Somewhere in between?

- Recite the words as if telling a story. Do it in a mirror or on your phone in camera mode.

- Without singing, could someone still tell what you were singing about?

- Now, let's sing the song with the song video. Sing either part 1 or part 2 when the music divides into two parts.

- Record yourself singing along on your phone's camera. Are you expressive?

- Bonus: can you tap your feet to the beat?

- Good job!

Happy
from DESPICABLE ME 2
LEAD SHEET

Words and Music by PHARRELL WILLIAMS
Adapted and Arranged by JANET DAY

Clap a-long _ if _ you know _ what hap-pi-ness is to you.

hap - py. _____ be-cause I'm

Clap a-long if you feel _ like that's what you wan - na do.

hap - py. _____

All
mf
Here come bad news _ talk-in' this and that. Yeah!

Well, gim-me all ya got, _ and don't hold it back. Yeah!

Well, I should prob-'bly warn _ you I'll be just fine. Yeah!

Spoken   **Part 2**
                              f
No of-fense to you, _ don't waste your time. Here's why! Be-cause I'm

Part 1
f
Clap a-long if you feel like a room with-out a roof.

hap - py. _____ be-cause I'm

high! Bring me down, ___ can't noth-in' Bring me down,

hap-py, hap-py, hap-py, hap-py, hap-py, hap-py, hap-py. Be-cause I'm

Clap a-long if ___ you feel ___ like a room with-out a roof.

hap-py. _____ be-cause I'm

Clap a-long if ___ you feel ___ like hap-pi-ness is the truth.

hap-py. _____ be-cause I'm

Clap a-long ___ if ___ you know ___ what hap-pi-ness is to you.

hap-py. _____ be-cause I'm

Clap a-long if ___ you feel ___ like that's what you wan-na do.

hap-py. _____

Happy

LYRICS

It might seem crazy what I'm 'bout to say.
Sunshine she's here, you can take a break.
I'm a hot air balloon that could go to space,
With the air, like I don't care, baby by the way.
Here's why!

Because I'm happy,
(Clap along if you feel like a room without a roof.)
Because I'm happy.
(Clap along if you feel like happiness is the truth.)
Because I'm happy,
(Clap along if you know what happiness is to you.)
Because I'm happy.
(Clap along if you feel like that's what you wanna do.)

Here come bad news talkin' this and that.
Yeah! Well gimme all ya got, and don't hold it back.
Yeah! Well I should prob'bly warn you I'll be just fine.
Yeah! No offense to you, don't waste your time.
Here's why!

Because I'm happy,
(Clap along if you feel like a room without a roof.)
Because I'm happy.
(Clap along if you feel like happiness is the truth.)
Because I'm happy,
(Clap along if you know what happiness is to you.)
Because I'm happy.
(Clap along if you feel like that's what you wanna do.)

Bring me down, can't nothin'
Bring me down. My level's too high!
Bring me down, can't nothin'
Bring me down, I said.

Happy, happy, (Bring me down,)
Happy, happy, (Can't nothin')
Happy, happy, (Bring me down.)
Happy, happy, (My level's too high!)
Happy, happy, (Bring me down,)
Happy, happy, (Can't nothin')
Happy, happy, (Bring me down,)

Because I'm happy,
(Clap along if you feel like a room without a roof.)
Because I'm happy.
(Clap along if you feel like happiness is the truth.)
Because I'm happy,
(Clap along if you know what happiness is to you.)
Because I'm happy.
(Clap along if you feel like that's what you wanna do.)

Baby Shark ▶

DESCRIPTION & INSTRUCTION
Enunciation: Singing Words Clearly

- For a song to make sense, it is important to pronounce the words clearly.

- This is a fun song to practice using your *articulators*.

- Articulators are: the lips, the teeth, the tip of the tongue.

- Quickly say: the lips, the teeth, the tip of the tongue. Repeat four times in a row.

- Now use these articulators to sing "Baby Shark."

Baby Shark

LEAD SHEET

Traditional Nursery Rhyme
Arranged by PINKFONG and KIDZCASTLE

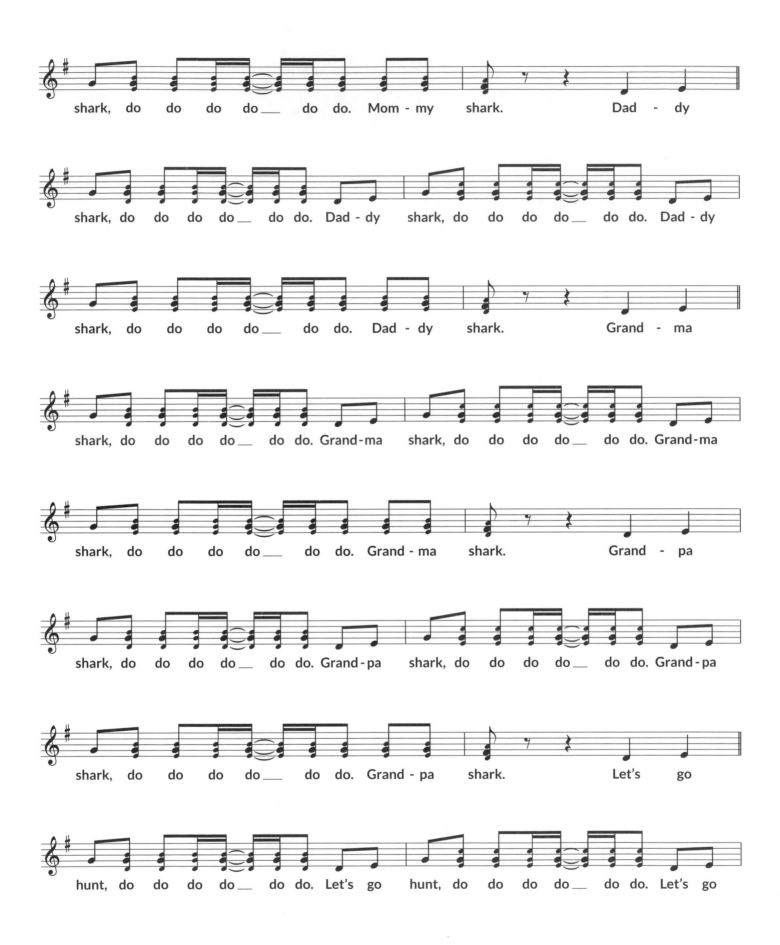

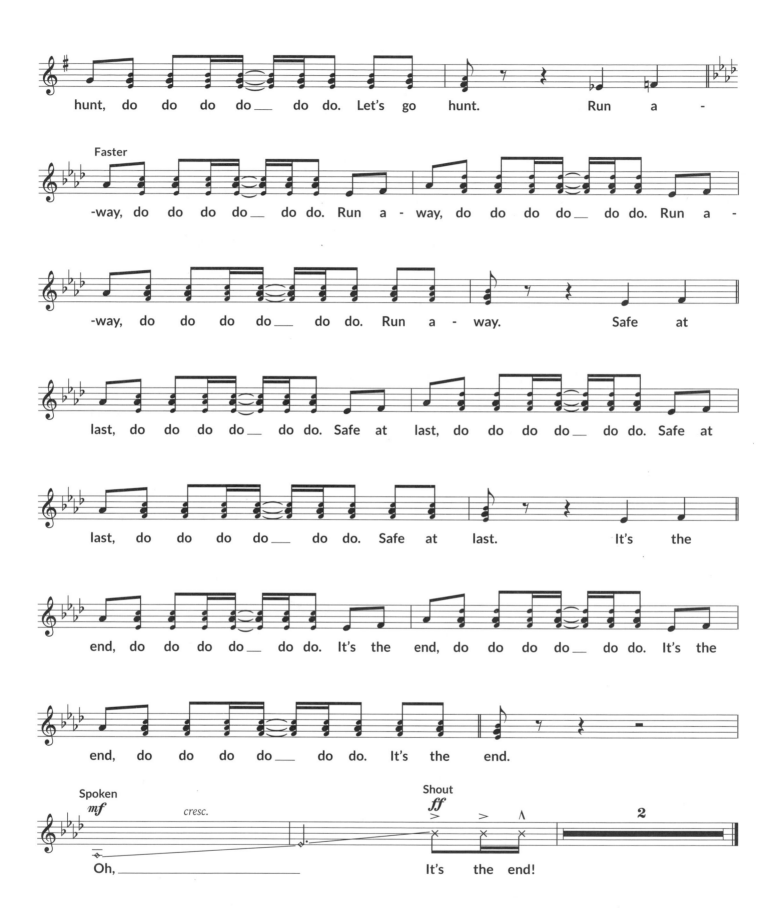

hunt, do do do do___ do do. Let's go hunt. Run a-

Faster

-way, do do do do___ do do. Run a-way, do do do do___ do do. Run a-

-way, do do do do___ do do. Run a-way. Safe at

last, do do do do___ do do. Safe at last, do do do do___ do do. Safe at

last, do do do do___ do do. Safe at last. It's the

end, do do do do___ do do. It's the end, do do do do___ do do. It's the

end, do do do do___ do do. It's the end.

Spoken *mf* *cresc.* **Shout** *ff* > > ∧ **2**

Oh,___ It's the end!

27

Baby Shark

LYRICS

Baby shark, do do do do do do.
Baby shark, do do do do do do.
Baby shark, do do do do do do.
Baby shark.

Mommy shark, do do do do do do.
Mommy shark, do do do do do do.
Mommy shark, do do do do do do.
Mommy shark.

Daddy shark, do do do do do do.
Daddy shark, do do do do do do.
Daddy shark, do do do do do do.
Daddy shark.

Grandma shark, do do do do do do.
Grandma shark, do do do do do do.
Grandma shark, do do do do do do.
Grandma shark.

Grandpa shark, do do do do do do.
Grandpa shark, do do do do do do.
Grandpa shark, do do do do do do.
Grandpa shark.

Let's go hunt, do do do do do do.
Let's go hunt, do do do do do do.
Let's go hunt, do do do do do do.
Let's go hunt.

Run away, do do do do do do.
Run away, do do do do do do.
Run away, do do do do do do.
Run away.

Safe at last, do do do do do do.
Safe at last, do do do do do do.
Safe at last, do do do do do do.
Safe at last.

It's the end, do do do do do do.
It's the end, do do do do do do.
It's the end, do do do do do do.
It's the end.

Oh, it's the end!

Lean On Me
Don't Stop Believin'

DESCRIPTION & INSTRUCTION
Reading Music: Singing Step by Step

- Singing step by step is the easiest kind of music reading.

- See how the first line of the song goes up like a ladder, and then down like a ladder.

- This "ladder of notes" is called a *scale*, which we learned about on page 9.

- Practice singing this line from "Lean on Me."

- What other song in this book goes up the scale? (Hint: it is a ballad.)
- Bonus: when two or more songs are put together, it is called a *medley*.

Lean On Me · Don't Stop Believin'
LEAD SHEET

Original Glee arrangements by
ADAM ANDERS and TIM DAVIS
Adapted for publication by JOHN HIGGINS

born and raised in south De - troit. _____ He took the

mid - night train __ go - in' an - y - where. __

cresc. poco a poco   *sim.*

Dah dah dah dah dah dah dah dah dah dah dah dah

dah dah dah dah dah dah dah dah dah dah dah dah

Driving
ff

dah dah dah dah dah dah dah dah Don't _ stop be -

liev - in'. Hold on to the feel - in', __ street - light

peo - ple. _____ Don't _ stop be -

liev - in'. Hold on to the feel - in', __ street - light

peo - ple. _____ Don't _ stop!

Lean On Me • Don't Stop Believin'
LYRICS

Hum, hum, hum, hum, hum,
Hum, hum, hum, hum,
Hum, hum, hum, hum, hum.
Hum, hum, hum, hum, hum,
Hum, hum, hum, hum,
Hum, hum, hum, hum, hum.

Sometimes in our lives we all have pain,
We all have sorrow.
But if we are wise, we know that there's
Always tomorrow.

Lean on me when you're not strong,
And I'll be your friend.
I'll help you carry on.
For it won't be long 'til I'm gonna need
Somebody to lean on.

Call on me, brother, when you need a hand.
We all need somebody to lean on.

We just might have a problem
That you'll understand.
We all need somebody to lean on.
Call me!

Dah dah dah dah
Dah dah dah dah
Dah dah dah dah
Dah dah dah dah

Dah dah dah dah
Dah dah dah dah
Dah dah dah dah
Dah dah dah dah

Just a small town girl, livin' in a lonely world.
She took the midnight train goin' anywhere.

Just a city boy, born and raised in south Detroit.
He took the midnight train goin' anywhere.

Dah dah dah dah
Dah dah dah dah
Dah dah dah dah
Dah dah dah dah

Dah dah dah dah
Dah dah dah dah
Dah dah dah dah
Dah dah dah dah

Don't stop belevin'.
Hold on to the feelin', Streetlight people.
Don't stop beleivin'.
Hold on to the feelin', Streetlight people.

Don't stop!

A Million Dreams

DESCRIPTION & INSTRUCTION
Reading Music: Singing by Leaps

- This song begins with a leap called a 4th, because it jumps up four notes of the scale.

- The leap is followed by two notes that move by step. (We learned singing by step on "Lean on Me.")

Words and Music by BENJ PASEK
and JUSTIN PAUL

'Cause ev - 'ry night __ I lie ____ in bed, __

- The next line starts with a leap of a 3rd (three notes), then two notes by step.

Words and Music by BENJ PASEK
and JUSTIN PAUL

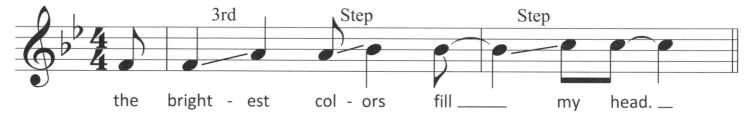

the bright - est col - ors fill ____ my head. __

- Good job! You are learning to *sight sing* music!

A Million Dreams
from THE GREATEST SHOWMAN
LEAD SHEET

Words and Music by
BENJ PASEK and JUSTIN PAUL

Flowing

Opt. Solo

I close my eyes __ and I can see __ a world that's wait- -ing up for me, __ that I call my own.

Through the dark, __ through the door, __ through where no __ one's been __ be - fore, __ but it feels like home.

They can say, they can say it all __ sounds cra - zy __ They can say, they can say I've lost __ my mind. __

I don't care, I don't care, so call me cra - zy. __ We can live in a world that we __ de - sign. __

'Cause ev - 'ry night __ I lie __ in bed, __ the bright-est col-ors fill __ my head. __ A mil - lion dreams __ are keep- -in' me __ a - wake. __

I think of what __ the world __ could be, __ a

vi-sion of＿ the one＿ I see.＿ A mil-lion dreams＿ is all＿ it's gon-na take,＿

Opt. Solo

mp

oh, a mil-lion dreams＿ for the world we're gon-na make.

4

All *mp*

There's a house＿

＿ we can build, ＿ Ev - 'ry room ＿ in - side ＿ is filled ＿ with

things from far ＿＿＿＿ a - way. ＿ Spe - cial things ＿ I com-pile, ＿

cresc.

＿ each ＿ one there ＿ to make ＿ you smile ＿ on a rain - y day.

mf

They can say, they can say it all＿sounds cra - zy. ＿＿＿

They can say, they can say we've lost ＿ our minds. ＿ I don't care, I don't

care if they call us cra - zy. ＿＿＿ Run a-way to a world that we＿ de - sign. ＿

cresc.

f

＿＿＿＿ Ev - 'ry night ＿ I lie ＿ in bed, ＿ the bright-est col-ors fill＿

_ my head. _ A mil - lion dreams _ are keep - in' me _ a - wake. _

I think of what _ the world _ could be, _ a vi-sion of _ the one _

_ I see. _ A mil-lion dreams _ is all _ it's gon-na take, _ oh, a

mil - lion dreams _ for the world we're gon - na make. 'Cause

ev - 'ry night _ I lie _ in bed, _ the bright-est col-ors fill _ my head. _ A

mil - lion dreams _ are keep - in' me _ a - wake. _ I

think of what _ the world _ could be, _ a vi-sion of _ the one _ I see. _ A

mil-lion dreams _ is all _ it's gon-na take, _ A mil-lion dreams _ for the

world we're gon - na make, _

molto rit. _mp_ Slowly, freely _a tempo_ _rit._ **5**

for the world we're gon - na make. _

A Million Dreams

LYRICS

I close my eyes and I can see
A world that's waiting up for me,
That I call my own.
Through the dark, through the door,
Through where no one's been before,
But it feels like home.

They can say, they can say it all sounds crazy.
They can say, they can say I've lost my mind.
I don't care, I don't care, so call me crazy.
We can live in a world that we design.

'Cause every night I lie in bed,
The brightest colors fill my head.
A million dreams are keepin' me awake.
I think of what the world could be,
A vision of the one I see.
A million dreams is all it's gonna take,
Oh, a million dreams for the world we're gonna make.

There's a house we can build,
Every room inside is filled
With things from far away.
Special things I compile,
Each one there to make you smile
On a rainy day.

They can say, they can say it all sounds crazy.
They can say, they can say we've lost our minds.
I don't care, I don't care, if they call us crazy.
Run away to a world that we design.

Every night I lie in bed,
The brightest colors fill my head.
A million dreams are keepin' me awake.
I think of what the world could be,
A vision of the one I see.
A million dreams is all it's gonna take,
Oh, a million dreams for the world we're gonna make.

'Cause every night I lie in bed,
The brightest colors fill my head.
A million dreams are keepin' me awake.
I think of what the world could be,
A vision of the one I see.
A million dreams is all it's gonna take,
A million dreams for the world we're gonna make,
For the world we're gonna make.

Dynamite ▶

DESCRIPTION & INSTRUCTION

Tone: Singing *Tall* Vowels

- Fun fact: song titles cannot be copyrighted. The same song title is used in the BTS hit, "Dynamite."

- Dynamite has several words that will sound better with a *tall* vowel.

- A tall vowel is the shape of your mouth when you sing the "oo," "oh," and "ah" sounds.

- Practice this tall "ah" vowel on the word "on." Open your mouth wide (like eating a hot potato). "And it goes ON and ON and ON, and it goes ON and ON and ON, yeah."

- Bonus: can you tap the beat?

Dynamite
LEAD SHEET

Words and Music by TAIO CRUZ, LUKASZ GOTTWALD,
MAX MARTIN, BENJAMIN LEVIN and BONNIE MCKEE
Adapted by JANET DAY

move, move, move, move. Get out the way _ me and my crew, crew, crew, crew.

I'm in the groove, _ I'm gon-na do, do, do, do just what we all _ came here to

do, do, do, do. Yeah, yeah, 'cause it goes on and on _ and on, _

_ and it goes on and on _ and on, _ yeah. _

I throw my hands up in the air some - times, say - in' ay - oh, got - ta

let go. I wan - na cel - e - brate and live my _ life, say - in'

ay - oh, ba - by, let's go. 'Cause we gon' rock this _ club, we gon'

go all _ night. We gon' light it _ up like it's dy - na - mite. 'Cause I

told you _ once, now I told you _ twice, we gon' light it _ up like it's

dy - na - mite. I'm gon - na take it all, _ I,

I'm gon - na be the last _ one stand - ing. High - er o - ver all, _

Dynamite

LYRICS

I came to dance, dance, dance, dance.
I hit the floor 'cause that's my plans, plans, plans, plans.
I'm wearing all my fav'rite brands, brands, brands, brands.
Give me some space for both my hands, hands, hands, hands.

You, you, 'cause it goes on and on and on,
And it goes on and on and on, yeah.

I throw my hands up in the air sometimes,
Sayin' ay-oh, gotta let go.
I wanna celebrate and live my life,
Sayin' ay-oh, baby let's go.

'Cause we gon' rock this club, we gon' go all night.
We gon' light it up like it's dynamite.
'Cause I told you once, now I told you twice,
We gon' light it up like it's dynamite.

I came to move, move, move, move.
Get out the way me and my crew, crew, crew, crew.
I'm in the groove, I'm gonna do, do, do, do
Just what we all came here to do, do, do, do.

Yeah, yeah, 'cause it goes on and on and on,
And it goes on and on and on, yeah.

I throw my hands up in the air sometimes,
Sayin' ay-oh, gotta let go.
I wanna celebrate and live my life,
Sayin' ay-oh, baby let's go.

'Cause we gon' rock this club, we gon' go all night.
We gon' light it up like it's dynamite.
'Cause I told you once, now I told you twice,
We gon' light it up like it's dynamite.

I'm gonna take it all,
I, I'm gonna be the last one standing
Higher over all,
I, I'm gonna be the last one landing
'Cause I, I, I believe it,
And I, I, I, I just want it all
I just want it all.
I'm gonna put my hands in the air,
Ha-hands in the air.
Put your hands in the air,
Yeah, yeah, yeah, yeah,
Yeah, yeah, yeah, yeah.

I throw my hands up in the air sometimes,
Sayin' ay-oh, gotta let go.
I wanna celebrate and live my life,
Sayin' ay-oh, baby let's go.

'Cause we gon' rock this club, we gon' go all night.
We gon' light it up like it's dynamite.
'Cause I told you once, now I told you twice,
We gon' light it up like it's dynamite.

Let It Go
from FROZEN

DESCRIPTION & INSTRUCTION
Adding Interest: Dynamics

- Fun fact: "Let It Go" was written during a walk in the park. When presented to the *Frozen* movie creators, they had to rewrite the theme of the movie to fit the song.

- Dynamics are a simply singing loud, soft, or in between.

- Your songs will sound better if you vary singing soft and then loud.

- "Let It Go" starts softly and then builds to loud at the end.

- *mp* means *mezzo piano*, or medium soft.

- *cresc.* stands for *crescendo*, or get gradually louder.

- *f* means *forte*, or loud.

- Bonus: *sub.* stands for *subito*, which means suddenly. *sub. mp* means suddenly sing medium soft.

Let It Go
from FROZEN
LEAD SHEET

Music and Lyrics by
KRISTEN ANDERSON-LOPEZ and ROBERT LOPEZ
Arranged by TOM ANDERSON

going to __ say; __ let the storm rage _ on. ____ The

Gaining confidence
2 *mf*

cold nev-er both-ered me an - y-way. It's fun-ny how some dis - tance makes

ev - 'ry-thing _ seem small; __ and the fears that once _ con - trolled __ me can't

get to me __ at all. __ It's time _ to see __ what I __ can do,

cresc.

to test _ the lim - its and _ break through. __ No right, _ no wrong, _

f

_ no rules _ for me; __ I'm free! _____ Let it go, __ let it go; _

I am one with the wind and sky. __ Let it go, __ let it go; _

you'll _ nev - er see ___ me _ cry. _ Here I stand, _

and here I'll __ stay; __ let the storm rage _ on. _

opt. Solo
*sub. **mp***
2

_____ The cold nev-er both-ered me an - y-way.

Let It Go
from FROZEN
LYRICS

The snow glows white on the mountain tonight;
Not a footprint to be seen
A kingdom of isolation
And it looks like I'm the queen.
The wind is howling like the swirling storm inside.
Couldn't keep it in;
Heaven knows I tried.

Don't let them in; don't let them see;
Be the good girl you always have to be.
Conceal, don't feel, don't let them know…
Well, now they know.

Let it go, let it go;
Can't hold it back anymore.
Let it go, let it go;
Turn away and slam the door.
I don't care what they're going to say;
Let the storm rage on.
The cold never bothered me anyway.

It's funny how some distance
Makes ev'rything seem small;
And the fears that once controlled me
Can't get to me at all.

It's time to see what I can do,
To test the limits and break through.
No right, no wrong, no rules for me;
I'm free!

Let it go, let it go;
I am one with the wind and sky.
Let it go, let it go;
You'll never see me cry.
Here I stand, and here I'll stay;
Let the storm rage on.
The cold never bothered me anyway.

Under the Sea ▶
from THE LITTLE MERMAID

DESCRIPTION & INSTRUCTION

Lyrics: Words are Important

- This song has very clever lyrics.

- Read them aloud before singing them.

- Tell the story when singing the words, making some lyrics louder than others, just like you do when telling a story to your friends.

- Try this: "The seaweed is always greener, IN SOMEBODY ELSE'S LAKE!"

- Bonus: watch *Howard* on Disney+ about the man who wrote the lyrics.

Under the Sea
from THE LITTLE MERMAID
LEAD SHEET

Music by ALAN MENKEN
Lyrics by HOWARD ASHMAN

The sea - weed is al - ways green - er in some - bod - y el - se's lake. You dream a-bout go - ing up there, but that is a big mis - take. Just look at the world a - round you, right here on the o - cean floor. Such won - der - ful things sur-round you, what more is you look - in' for? Un - der the sea, un - der the sea, dar - lin' it's bet-ter down where it's wet-ter, take it from me. Up on the shore they work all day. Out in the sun they slave a - way, while we de - vo - tin' full time to

float-in' un - der the sea. Down here _ all the fish is hap - py,

as off _ through the waves they roll. The fish _ on the land ain't hap - py.

They sad _ 'cause they in the bowl. But fish _ in the bowl is luck - y,

they in __ for a worse - er fate. One day _ when the boss get hun - gry,

(Opt. Solo)

(All)

guess who _ gon' be on the plate? Un - der the sea,

un - der the sea, no - bod - y beat us, fry _ us and

eat us in __ fri - cas - see. _____ We _ what the land folks love _ to cook.

Un - der the sea we off __ the hook. We _ got no

trou-bles, life _ is the bub-bles un - der the sea.

Under the Sea
from THE LITTLE MERMAID
LYRICS

The seaweed is always greener
In somebody else's lake.
You dream about going up there,
But that is a big mistake.
Just look at the world around you,
Right here on the ocean floor.
Such wonderful things surround you,
What more is you lookin' for?

Under the sea, under the sea,
Darlin' it's better down where it's wetter, take it from me.
Up on the shore the work all day.
Out in the sun they slave away,
While we devotin' full time to floatin' under the sea.

Down here all the fish is happy,
As off through the waves they roll.
The fish on the land ain't happy.
They say 'cause they in the bowl.
But fish in the bowl is lucky,
They in for a worser fate.
One day when the boss get hungry,
Guess who gon' be on the plate?

Under the sea, under the sea,
Nobody beat us, fry us and eat us in fricassee.
We what the land folks love to cook.
Under the sea we off the hook.
We got no troubles, life is the bubbles under the sea.

Better When I'm Dancin'
from THE PEANUTS MOVIE

DESCRIPTION & INSTRUCTION
Song Form: Verse, Chorus, Bridge

- Fun fact: Meghan Trainor began singing at the age of 6 at her church. Her father was a music teacher and organist.

- Listen to the song.

- The *verse* tells the story.

- The *chorus* is the main theme of the song, which is repeated and often is the title of the song.

- Can you tell when the verse ends and the chorus begins?

- We call the verse the A section, and the chorus the B section.

- A *bridge* is a completely different section and it's called the C section. Not all songs have a bridge, but this one does. Can you find it?

- Bonus: let your body move to the music!

Better When I'm Dancin'
from THE PEANUTS MOVIE

LEAD SHEET

Words and Music by
MEGHAN TRAINOR and THADDEUS DIXON

danc - in',   yeah,   yeah. __   Bop __ ba da,   da   da   da   da

da   dut,   la   la   la   la   la   lut,   la   la   la   la   la   lut,   bop   ba   da   da.

mp

When you   fi - n'lly   let   go,   and   you   slay   that   so - lo,

'cause you   lis - ten   to   the   mu - sic,   sing - in',   "Oh,   aye   oh." __

__   'Cause you're con - fi - dent, babe,   and   you   make   your   hips   sway.

We knew that you could   do   it, __   sing, "Oh   aye   oh."   Show   the   world _   you   got   that

fi - re, __   feel   the   rhy - thm   get - ting   loud - er. __

Show   the   room _   what   you   can   do,   prove   to   them _   you   got   them

moves.   I don't know 'bout you, but I feel bet - ter when I'm   danc - in',   yeah,   yeah.

_   I'm   bet - ter   when   I'm   danc - in',   yeah,   yeah. _

And we _ can do   this   to - geth - er.   I   bet _ you feel bet - ter when you're

danc - in',   yeah,   yeah. _   Bop _ ba da,   da   da   da da

da dut,   la   la   la   la   la lut,   la   la   la   la   la lut,   bop ba da da.

Bop _ ba da,   da da da da   da dut,   la la la la   la lut,   la la la la

la lut,   bop ba da da.   Oh   aye   oh. __   Oh   aye   oh. __

_   I feel bet - ter when I'm   yeah, _   yeah. __

58

Better When I'm Dancin'
from THE PEANUTS MOVIE
LYRICS

Don't think about it, just move your body
Listen to the music, sing, "Oh aye oh."
Just move those left feet. Go ahead, get crazy.
Anyone can do it, sing, "Oh aye oh."

Show the world you got that fire,
Feel the rhythm getting louder.
Show the room what you can do,
Prove to them you got them moves.
I don't know 'bout you,

But I feel better when I'm dancin', yeah, yeah.
I'm better when I'm dancin', yeah, yeah.
And we can do this together.
I bet you feel better when you're dancing', yeah, yeah.

Bop ba da, da da da da da dut,
La la la la la lut,
La la la la la lut,
Bop ba da da.

When you fin'lly let go, and you slay that solo,
'Cause you listen to the music, singin', "Oh, aye oh."
'Cause your confident, babe, and you make your hips sway.
We knew that you could do it, sing, "Oh, aye oh."
Show the world you got that fire,
Feel the rhythm getting louder.
Show the room what you can do,
Prove to them you got them moves.
I don't know 'bout you,

But I feel better when I'm dancin', yeah, yeah.
I'm better when I'm dancin', yeah, yeah.
And we can do this together.
I bet you feel better when you're dancing', yeah, yeah.

Bop ba da, da da da da da dut,
La la la la la lut,
La la la la la lut,
Bop ba da da.

Bop ba da, da da da da da dut,
La la la la la lut,
La la la la la lut,
Bop ba da da.

Oh aye oh.
Oh aye oh.
I feel better when I'm
Yeah, yeah.

You Raise Me UP ▶️

DESCRIPTION & INSTRUCTION

Phrasing: Singing a Musical Sentence

- This song is a ballad.

- A ballad is usually slow and tells a story.

- Each sentence (phrase) should be sung in one breath. Don't take a breath in the middle of a phrase.

- Take a deep breath before singing a phrase so you have plenty of air to complete it.

- Crescendo (get louder) in the middle of each phrase to make it sound more interesting. Then soften (decrescendo) near the end.

You Raise Me Up

LEAD SHEET

Words and Music by
BRENDAN GRAHAM and ROLF LOVLAND
Arranged by JANET DAY

moun - tains. You raise me up to walk on storm - y seas. I am

strong when I am on ___ your shoul - ders. You raise me

up to more than I ___ can be. You raise me

up so I can stand on moun - tains. You raise me

up to walk on storm - y seas. I am

strong when I am on ___ your shoul - ders. You raise me

dim. *mf*

up to more than I ___ can be. ___ You raise me

rit. *mp*

up to more than I ___ can

be. ___

You Raise Me UP
LYRICS

When I am down and oh, my soul, so weary,
When troubles come and my heart burdened be,
Then I am still and wait here in the silence
Until you come and sit a while with me.

You raise me up so I can stand on mountains.
You raise me up to walk on stormy seas.
I am strong when I am on your shoulders.
You raise me up to more than I can be.

You raise me up so I can stand on mountains.
You raise me up to walk on stormy seas.
I am strong when I am on your shoulders.
You raise me up to more than I can be.

You raise me up so I can stand on mountains.
You raise me up to walk on stormy seas.
I am strong when I am on your shoulders.
You raise me up to more than I can be.
You raise me up to more than I can be.

Count on Me ▶

DESCRIPTION & INSTRUCTION

The Groove: Rock vs. Swing

- Most songs have either a *rock* feel or a *swing* feel. It's called the groove.

- Rock feel uses even rhythms. Listen to "Better When I'm Dancing" or "Lean on Me" for an example.

- "Count on Me" uses uneven rhythms called *triplets*. It has a swing feel.

- Notice how it feels like skipping. Long short, long short, long short.

- *Shuffle* is a special kind of swing used in this song.

- Bonus: is this a happy song? Do your face and eyes show it?

Count on Me

LEAD SHEET

Words and Music by BRUNO MARS,
ARI LEVINE and PHILIP LAWRENCE
Arranged by JANET DAY

Uh _ huh. _ If you ev-er find your-self stuck in the mid-dle of the sea, I'll sail the world _ to find _ you. If you ev-er find your-self lost in the dark, and you can't see, I'll be the light _ to guide _ you. We find out what _ we're made of _____ when we are called _ to help our friends _ in need. You can count on me like "one, two, three." I'll be _____ there, and I know when I need it, I can count on you like "four, three, two," and you'll be _ there, 'cause that's what friends _ are s'posed to do, _ oh, yeah.

Oo, _____ oo, _____ yeah,

yeah. If you're toss-in' and your turn-in' and you just can't fall a - sleep,

I'll sing a song _ be - side _ you. If you

ev - er for - get how much you real - ly mean to me, ev - 'ry

day I will _ re - mind _ you. We

find out what _ we're made of _____ when we are called _ to

help our friends _ in need. You can count on me like

"one, two, three." I'll be _____ there, and I know when I

need it, I can count on you like "four, three, two," and you'll be _

_ there, 'cause that's what friends _ are s'posed to do, _ oh, yeah.

Oo, _____ oo, _____ yeah,

yeah. You'll al - ways have my shoul - der when you cry. ____

_____ I'll nev - er let go, nev - er

say good - bye. ____ You know you can __ count on

me like "one, two, three." I'll be __ there, and

I know when I need it, I can count on you like "four, three,

two," and you'll be __ there, 'cause that's what friends __ are

s'posed to do, _ oh, yeah. Oo, _____ oo, _____

_____ You can count on me, ___ 'cause

I can count _ on you. _____

Count on Me

LYRICS

Uh huh.
If you ever find yourself stuck in the middle of the sea,
I'll sail the world to find you.
If you ever find yourself lost in the dark, and you can't see,
I'll be the light to guide you.
We find out what we're made of
When we are called to help our friends in need.

You can count on me like "one, two, three."
I'll be there,
And I know when I need it,
I can count on you like "four, three, two,"
And you'll be there,
'Cause that's what friends are s'posed to do, oh, yeah.
Oo, oo, yeah, yeah.

If you're tossin' and you're turnin' and you just can't fall asleep,
I'll sing a song beside you.
If you ever forget how much you really mean to me,
Ev'ry day I will remind you.
We find out what we're made of
When we are called to help our friends in need.

You can count on me like "one, two, three."
I'll be there,
And I know when I need it,
I can count on you like "four, three, two,"
And you'll be there,
'Cause that's what friends are s'posed to do, oh, yeah.
Oo, oo, yeah, yeah.

You'll always have my shoulder when you cry.
I'll never let go, never say goodbye.

You know you can count on me like "one, two, three."
I'll be there,
And I know when I need it,
I can count on you like "four, three, two,"
And you'll be there,
'Cause that's what friends are s'posed to do, oh, yeah.
Oo, oo,
You can count on me, 'cause I can count on you.

Hallelujah
from the Motion Picture SING

DESCRIPTION & INSTRUCTION

Range: Singing High and Low

- Fun Fact: There are over 100 verses to this song! The most popular are included in this version.

- This song uses lots of notes, both high and low.

- Most of the song is sung in the low or *chest voice*. Notice how the notes are lower on the music staff.

- Toward the end of the song, you need to sing in the upper voice called your head voice. The notes are higher on the music staff.

- Practice the warmups in Exercises 5 and 6 (on the video and on page 15) to help you build your full range of singing notes

- Bonus: what expression did you use on your face?

- Bonus: is the tempo of the beat slow or fast?

Hallelujah
from the Motion Picture SING
LEAD SHEET

Moderately slow

Words and Music by LEONARD COHEN

more intensity

There's a blaze of light in ev - 'ry word. It does - n't mat - ter

what you heard, _ the ho - ly or the bro - ken hal - le - lu - jah.

melody
mp

Hal - le - lu - jah!   Hal - le - lu - jah!   Hal - le - lu - jah!

opt. harmony
mp

Hal - le - lu - jah!   Hal - le - lu - jah!   Hal - le - lu - jah!

mp

Hal - le - lu - jah!   I

Hal - le - lu - jah!

gradually build intensity

did my best, _ it was - n't much. _ I could - n't feel, _ so I

mp   *gradually build intensity*

Oo, _____ oo, _____

tried to touch. I've told the truth, I did - n't __ come to fool ya. __

_ oo. _____

Hallelujah
from the Motion Picture SING
LYRICS

Now I've heard there was a secret chord
That David played and it pleased the Lord,
But you don't really care for music, do you?
It goes like this: the fourth, the fifth,
The minor fall and the major lift.
The baffled king composing "Hallelujah."

Hallelujah!
Hallelujah!
Hallelujah!
Hallelujah!

You say I took the name in vain.
I don't even know the Name,
But if I did, well, really, what's it to you?
There's a blaze of light in ev'ry word.
It dosen't matter what you heard.
The holy or the broken hallelujah.

Hallelujah!
Hallelujah!
Hallelujah!
Hallelujah!

I did my best, it wasn't much.
I couldn't feel, so I tried to touch.
I've told the truth, I didn't come to fool ya.
And even though it all went wrong,
I'll stand before the Lord of song
With nothing on my tongue but "Hallelujah."

Hallelujah!
Hallelujah!
Hallelujah!
Hallelu!

Hallelujah!
Hallelujah!
Hallelujah!
Hallelu.
Hallelujah!

Christmas Time Is Here ▶

from A CHARLIE BROWN CHRISTMAS

DESCRIPTION & INSTRUCTION

Time Signatures – 4/4 and 3/4.

- Most songs are in 4/4 time with a steady beat in groups of four. 1-2-3-4, 1-2-3-4, etc.

- This song is in 3/4 with a steady beat in groups of three. 1-2-3, 1-2-3, etc.

- It is also called *waltz time,* after the dance. It has a slight bounce called a *lilt.*

- This sing is called a *jazz waltz* because it has cool, jazzy chords in the accompaniment and is in 3/4 time.

- Bonus: what other holiday songs do you know?

Christmas Time Is Here
from A CHARLIE BROWN CHRISTMAS

LEAD SHEET

Words by LEE MENDELSON
Music by VINCE GUARALDI
Arranged by TOM ANDERSON

Christmas Time Is Here
from A CHARLIE BROWN CHRISTMAS
LYRICS

Christmas time is here,
Happiness and cheer.
Fun for all that children call
Their fav'rite time of year.

Snowflakes in the air,
Carols ev'rywhere.
Olden times and ancient rhythms
Of love and dreams to share.

Sleighbells in the air,
Beauty ev'rywhere.
Yuletide by the fireside
And joyful mem'ries there.

Christmas time is here, (Christmas time is here.)
We'll be drawing near. (We'll be drawing near.)
Oh, that we could always see
Such spirit through the year.

Oh, that we could always see
Such spirit through the year.
Oh, that we could always see
Such spirit through the year.
Oo, oo, oo.

HAL LEONARD METHODS FOR KIDS

This popular series of method books for youngsters provides accessible courses that teach children to play their instrument of choice faster than ever before. The clean, simple page layouts ensure kids' attention remains on each new concept. Every new song presented builds on concepts they have learned in previous songs, so kids stay motivated and progress with confidence. These methods can be used in combination with a teacher or parent. The price of each book includes access to audio play-along and demonstration tracks online for download or streaming.

GUITAR FOR KIDS, METHOD BOOK 1
by Bob Morris and Jeff Schroedl

This method is equally suitable for students using electric or acoustic guitars. It features popular songs, including: Hokey Pokey • Hound Dog • I'm a Believer • Surfin' USA • This Land Is Your Land • Yellow Submarine • and more.

00865003 Book/Online Audio.............................$14.99

GUITAR FOR KIDS, METHOD BOOK 2
by Chad Johnson

Equally suitable for children using electric or acoustic guitars, this book picks up where Book 1 left off. Songs include: Dust in the Wind • Eight Days a Week • Fields of Gold • Let It Go • Oye Como Va • Rock Around the Clock • and more.

00128437 Book/Online Audio.............................$14.99

GUITAR FOR KIDS: BLUES METHOD BOOK
by Dave Rubin

Cool blues riffs, chords and solos are featured in this method, which is suitable for children using electric or acoustic guitars. Lessons include: selecting your guitar • parts of the guitar • holding the guitar • hand position • easy tablature • strumming & picking • blues riffs & chords • basic blues soloing • and more.

00248636 Book/Online Audio.............................$14.99

GUITAR FOR KIDS SONGBOOK

This supplement follows chords in the order they are taught in book 1 of the guitar method. 10 songs: At the Hop • Don't Worry, Be Happy • Electric Avenue • Every Breath You Take • Feelin' Alright • Fly like an Eagle • Jambalaya (On the Bayou) • Love Me Do • Paperback Writer • Three Little Birds.

00697402 Book/Online Audio.............................$12.99

GUITAR FOR KIDS METHOD & SONGBOOK

00697403 Book/Online Audio.............................$22.99

Prices, contents, and availability subject to change without notice.

BASS FOR KIDS METHOD BOOK
by Chad Johnson

Topics in this method book include selecting a bass, holding the bass, hand position, reading music notation and counting, and more. It also features popular songs including: Crazy Train • Every Breath You Take • A Hard Day's Night • Wild Thing • and more. Includes tab.

00696449 Book/Online Audio.............................$14.99

DRUMS FOR KIDS METHOD BOOK

Topics included in this method book for young beginning drummers include setting up the drumset, music reading, learning rhthms, coordination, and more. Includes the songs: Another One Bites the Dust • Crazy Train • Free Fallin' • Living After Midnight • Old Time Rock & Roll • Stir It Up • When the Levee Breaks • and more.

00113420 Book/Online Audio.............................$14.99

HARMONICA FOR KIDS METHOD BOOK
by Eric Plahna

Lessons include topics such as hand position, basic chord playing, learning melodies, and much more. Includes over 30 songs: All My Loving • Happy Birthday to You • Jingle Bells • Over the River and Through the Woods • Scarborough Fair • Take Me Out to the Ball Game • This Land Is Your Land • You Are My Sunshine • and more.

00131101 Book/Online Audio.............................$14.99

PIANO FOR KIDS METHOD BOOK
by Jennifer Linn

This fun, easy course incorporates popular songs including: Beauty and the Beast • Heart and Soul • Let It Go • Over the Rainbow • We Will Rock You • and more classical/folk tunes. Topics covered include parts of the piano, good posture and hand position, note reading, dynamics and more.

00156774 Book/Online Audio.............................$13.99

PIANO FOR KIDS SONGBOOK
by Jennifer Linn

A supplementary companion to the method book for piano, this book presents classic songs and contemporary hits which progress in like manner with the method book. Includes: All of Me • Can't Stop the Feeling • Do Re Mi • Linus and Lucy • and more.

00217215 Book/Online Audio.............................$12.99

PIANO FOR KIDS CHRISTMAS SONGBOOK
by Jennifer Linn

Includes: Go, Tell It on the Mountain • I Want a Hippopotamus for Christmas • Jingle Bell Rock • Jingle Bells • Mary, Did You Know? • Rudolph the Red-Nosed Reindeer • Up on the Housetop • We Three Kings of Orient Are • and more.

00238915 Book/Online Audio.............................$12.99

UKULELE FOR KIDS
by Chad Johnson

This book features popular songs including: Barbara Ann • The Hokey Pokey • Rock Around the Clock • This Land Is Your Land • Yellow Submarine • You Are My Sunshine • and more. Lessons include: selecting your uke; parts of the uke; holding the uke; hand position; reading music notation and counting; notes on the strings; strumming and picking; and more!

00696468 Book/Online Audio.............................$14.99

UKULELE FOR KIDS SONGBOOK

Strum your favorite hits from Jason Mraz, Disney, U2 and more! This collection can be used on its own, as a supplement to the *Ukulele for Kids* method book or any other beginning ukulele method. Songs: Don't Worry, Be Happy • I'm Yours • The Lion Sleeps Tonight • Riptide • The Siamese Cat Song • and more.

00153137 Book/Online Audio.............................$12.99

UKULELE FOR KIDS METHOD & SONGBOOK

00244855 Book/Online Audio.............................$22.99

www.halleonard.com